Test Your Professional English

Business: General

Steve Flinders

Series Editor: Nick Brieger

PENGUIN ENGLISH

Pearson Education Limited
Edinburgh Gate
Harlow
Essex CM20 2JE, England
and Associated Companies throughout the world.

ISBN 0 582 45148 5

First published 1996 as *Test Your Business English Elementary*
This edition published 2002
Text copyright © Steve Flinders 1996, 2002

Designed and typeset by Pantek Arts Ltd, Maidstone, Kent
Text Your format devised by Peter Watcyn-Jones
Illustrations by Roger Fereday and Anthony Seldon
Printed in Italy by Rotolito Lombarda

Acknowledgements
Many thanks to John Fagan and Bob Dignen at York Associates for their advice on the content of this edition, and to Mathieu and Jérôme Flinders for their help with the proofs.

Published by Pearson Education Limited in association with Penguin Books Ltd, both companies being subsidiaries of Pearson plc.

For a complete list of the titles available from Penguin English please visit our website at www.penguinenglish.com, or write to your local Pearson Education office or to: Marketing Department, Penguin Longman Publishing, 80 Strand, London WC2R 0RL.

Contents

Section 8: General business

To the student

Do you work in business and use English in your job? Or are you a business student? Whatever your background, if you need to improve your business English, the tests in this book will help. They will check your knowledge of basic business words and essential business expressions so that you can understand and communicate more effectively and confidently.

There are eight sections in the book. The first section tests your ability to talk about yourself and your role: to say who you are and what you do. The other seven sections each cover a different area of business – from organization and different areas of business-to-business language and communication. You can work through the book from beginning to end, or you can work first on the tests which are most important to you.

Many tests also have tips (advice) on language and language learning, and information about business. Do read these explanations and tips: they are there to help you.

To make the book more challenging and more fun, many different kinds of test are used, including gap-filling, word families, multiple choice and crosswords. There is a key at the back of the book so that you can check your answers; and a word list to help you revise key vocabulary.

Your vocabulary is an essential resource for effective communication. It is important to remember that the more words you know, the more you can say and the more you can understand. These tests can help you check what you know and develop your knowledge of new concepts and terms in a structured and systematic way. This book can help you significantly increase your business vocabulary.

Steve Flinders

The full series consists of:

Test Your Professional English: Accounting	Alison Pohl
Test Your Professional English: Business General	Steve Flinders
Test Your Professional English: Business Intermediate	Steve Flinders
Test Your Professional English: Finance	Simon Sweeney
Test Your Professional English: Hotel and Catering	Alison Pohl
Test Your Professional English: Law	Nick Brieger
Test Your Professional English: Management	Simon Sweeney
Test Your Professional English: Marketing	Simon Sweeney
Test Your Professional English: Medical	Alison Pohl
Test Your Professional English: Secretarial	Alison Pohl

1 Your job

Complete each of the following sentences with *in*, *on* or *for*. There are two possible answers for number 2. You can then make similar sentences about yourself and your job.

1 Olga Blanc is _____*in*_____ computers.

2 She has been working _____ a big computer company for five years.

3 She is based _____ Paris.

4 She works _____ the external communications department.

5 At the moment she is working _____ the design of the company's website.

6 She is responsible _____ the development of an important part of the site.

7 She is very interested _____ Website design.

8 She depends _____ the web and on personal contacts for new ideas.

9 She spends one or two hours every day on the Web getting information _____ all the latest developments.

10 She is happy because there is a big demand _____ good website designers at the moment.

- Tenses at work
  You use the present simple to talk, for example, about where you work or what you do: *I work ...*
  You use the present continuous to talk about current projects:
  I am working ...
- **External communications** means how the company communicates with the outside world. **Internal communications** means how people inside the company communicate with each other.

2 Your company

Fill in the missing words in the sentences below. Choose from the words in the box. You can then use similar sentences to talk about your company.

~~company~~   competitors   customers   employees   leader   products
profit   share   shareholders   share price   subsidiaries   turnover

---

1   I work for a _____company_____ called Kwikshoe.

2   Our main _____ are sports shoes.

3   Kwikshoe is a world _____ in the tennis shoe sector.

4   It has a national market _____ of 23%.

5   It has 2,500 _____ in this country.

6   It has seven _____ in five different countries.

7   Its main _____ are young people and people who do sport.

8   Its main _____ are in Britain and the USA.

9   Its main _____ are banks and pension funds.

10   Its _____ last year was $1.2 billion.

11   Its _____ last year was $16 million.

12   Its _____ today is $57.

If you are the number one in a market, sector or region, you can say:
We are the leader in the … sector …
We are the biggest … in the market.

If you are the number two or three, you can say:
We are a leader in the provision of …
We are the second / third / fourth biggest … in the region.

---

3 Your daily routine

Lorenza Müller is telling her partner about her day at the office. Match the beginning of each sentence on the left (1–13) with a phrase on the right (a–m). You can then make similar sentences to talk about your day at work.

1 I looked at _j_	**a**	the monthly figures to Mr Kazoulis.
2 I wrote ___	**b**	an appointment with a client.
3 I made ___	**c**	the minutes of the meeting.
4 I went to ___	**d**	a representative of the safety committee.
5 I took ___	**e**	the company magazine.
6 I fixed ___	**f**	three or four replies.
7 I met ___	**g**	two or three telephone calls.
8 I had ___	**h**	the office Christmas party with Cynthia.
9 I read ___	**i**	a $10 million deal.
10 I discussed ___	**j**	my e-mails.
11 I presented ___	**k**	lunch with Tom in Accounts.
12 I negotiated ___	**l**	tired but happy.
13 I came home ___	**m**	the weekly departmental meeting.

4 The people you talk to

Choose one word or phrase from the box to complete each sentence.

boss   Chief Executive Officer   colleague   customer
director   investor   leader   manager   opposite number
~~owner~~   shareholder   supplier

My name's John Power. Power Enterprises belongs to me. I'm the (1) _____owner_____ . I also manage the company myself. I'm the (2) _____ .

I'm John Power's sister. I sit on the Board of his company. I'm a (3) _____ .

I'm Mr Power's secretary.
He's my (4) _____ .

I hold equity in this company.
I am a (5) _____ .

John Power is a friend of mine. I have put some of my own money into Power Enterprises. I'm an
(6) _____ .

I buy things from this company.
I'm a (7) _____ .

This company buys things from me.
I'm a (8) _____ .

I'm the head of a team in the technical department.
I'm a team (9) _____ .

I have lunch every day with the woman at the desk
next to mine. She is my (10) _____ .

I'm the marketing director of Power Asia Pacific. Jim
Poom is the marketing director of Power Europe.
He's my (11) _____ .

I work for Power Enterprises. I head a department of
about 50 people. I'm a (12) _____ .

There is not a big difference between **customers** and **clients** and
sometimes both can be used. In general, people in shops are usually
customers, while businesses and professional people like lawyers and
accountants have clients.

Boss is an informal word, not something you will see on an organization
chart. The terms **superior** and **subordinate** were once used to talk about
people above and below you in the organization, but they are less common
today.

5 Your pay

You have just agreed your pay with the Board. Fill in the missing words in the sentences below.

> benefits bonus car expenses health insurance income
> pension rise ~~salary~~ stock option vouchers

---

1 Your base _____*salary*_____ will be $500,000 per year.

2 When you are 65, you will get a _____ of $400,000 per year.

3 But you will get many other _____ as well.

4 A _____ plan gives you shares in the company which you can sell at a profit if the price goes up.

5 You have an expensive company _____ .

6 You have unlimited travel and entertainment _____ .

7 You get free _____ .

8 You get free luncheon _____ which you can use in most restaurants in the city.

9 And you get a special _____ if the company's sales go up by more than 15% in the year.

10 So your total _____ next year could be more than a million pounds. Even so, you are thinking about asking for another _____ soon!

One of the benefits…

6 Your career

Tony Johansen tells us about his professional life but some of the letters are missing from the key words. Fill in the missing letters. Take care with the correct form of the verb. You can then make similar sentences about your own professional life story.

1 I guess my C A R E E R so far has not been very typical.

2 My first J __ __ was with Flat Earth Mechanics.

3 I S __ A __ T __ __ with them in 1975.

4 It was just after I had L __ F __ school.

5 My first job was in the office but I soon M __ V __ __ to the sales department. I knew then that I was born to be a salesman!

6 In 1980 I was P __ O __ O __ E __ to the position of sales manager.

7 But soon after that, the company went through a bad period and most of us were M __ D __ R __ D __ N __ A __ T.

8 It took me two weeks to find another job and at the beginning of 1981 I J __ I __ E __ Round Earth Mechanics.

9 This was a much more successful company and in 1990 I was A __ P __ I __ T __ __ to the post of national sales manager.

10 Things have been fine since then although I was almost F __ R __ __ once for paying my sales people too much commission.

11 I have no plans to R __ T __ R __ before I'm 60.

12 If someone O __ F __ R __ me a better job, I will think about it seriously!

7 Your computer

Match the parts of the computer (a–k) with the following terms (1–11).

1	keyboard	_k_
2	screen	____
3	CD-ROM drive	____
4	printer	____
5	mouse	____
6	disk drive	____
7	disk	____
8	monitor	____
9	scanner	____
10	loudspeakers	____
11	web camera	____

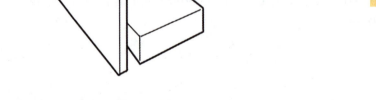

8 Your office

What do you keep on your desk and in your office? Match the items (a–o) with the correct terms (1–15).

1 ring binder   _c_

2 envelopes   _____

3 plastic sleeves   _____

4 Post-its   _____

5 scissors   _____

6 headed paper   _____

7 waste paper bin   _____

8 stapler   _____

9 staples   _____

10 in-tray   _____

11 filing cabinet   _____

12 hanging file   _____

13 paper clips   _____

14 ruler   _____

15 hole punch   _____

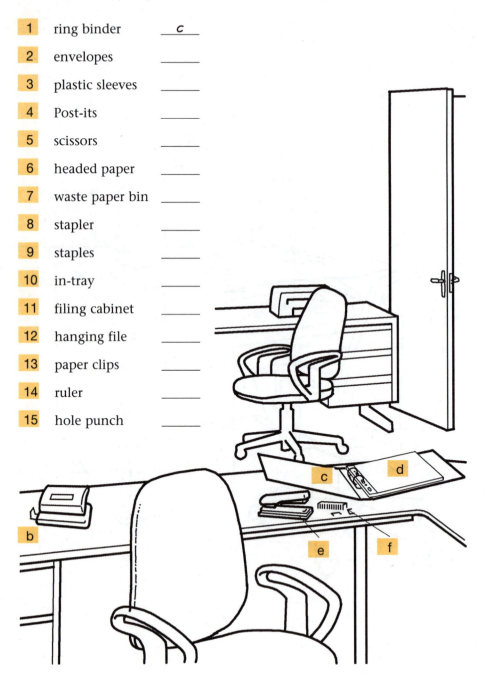

9 A visit to a business

Fill in the missing words or phrases in the sentences below. Use the pictures to help you. Choose from the words in the box. (When you have finished, you can say what visitors have to do to reach you.)

> appointment   badge   deal   floor   identity card
> lift   main building   ~~main gate~~   office   reception desk
> receptionist   secretary   security guard   sign

1

You arrive at the
_____main gate_____ .

2

You show your
_____ .

3

The _____
lets you go through.

4

You enter the
_____ .

5

You walk to the
_____ .

6

You give your name to
the _____ .

7

You have an

_____

with Mr Power at 9.

8

You _____

your name in the visitors'

book.

9

You pin your

_____

to your coat.

10

You find the

_____ .

11

You go to the top

_____ .

12

Mr Power's

_____

meets you.

13

She takes you to Mr Power's

_____ .

14

Mr Power says, 'Hi, we

have a _____ .'

British English speakers *take the **lift***.
American English speakers *take the **elevator***.

10 Places

Match the places (a–k) with the correct business locations (1–11).

1	call centre	_b_		7	research lab	_____
2	factory	_____		8	showroom	_____
3	meeting room	_____		9	trade fair	_____
4	office	_____		10	training centre	_____
5	open-plan office	_____		11	warehouse	_____
6	reception	_____				

a

b

c

d

11 Jobs

Match the business cards (a–l) with the job descriptions (1–12).

1 I buy all the things that the company needs. _f_

a

> **John Sutton**
> *Managing Director*

2 My job is to make sure that the company has a good image. _____

b

> Linda Gabbiadini
>
> Human Resources Director

3 My job is to find and test new products. _____

c

> **Dietrich Hoffmeister**
> **Finance Director**

4 I'm in charge of the people who sell our products. _____

d

> **Alice Hernandez**
>
> **Chief Accountant**

5 I type letters, file papers and make appointments for my boss. _____

e

> **Li Wan**   *Secretary*

6 I have general responsibility for the whole company. _____

f

> *LENA JOHANSSON*
> **PURCHASING MANAGER**

7 I make sure we have the products which people want to buy. _____

g
> ### *François Barbot*
>
> Assistant General Manager

8 I look after the company's money. _____

h
> ## YURI MANKOVICH
> **Director of Research**
> **and Development**

9 I do the books and prepare the balance sheets. _____

i
> ### Jim Hicks
> ### Production Manager

10 I'm the company's people manager. _____

j
> ### PADRIG BYRNE
> *MARKETING DIRECTOR*

11 I make the products which the company sells. _____

k
> Santi Brunello
>
> **Sales Director**

12 I'm responsible for everything when the boss is away. _____

l
> ### Kate Hogg
> Public Relations Manager

In some cultures, people exchange **business cards** at the beginning of a meeting or a visit. In others, they do it at the end of the meeting.

In some cultures, people present their business cards with one hand. In others, they present the card with two hands.

In some cultures, business cards are usually white. In others, they can be multi-coloured.

What information do you have on your card? What colour is it? When do you give it to another person? Do you know people who do things differently?

12 Grades

Square Hole Engineering Inc. has four white-collar grades and four blue-collar grades. Write the names of all eight grades in the list, from the top (1) to the bottom (8).

---

clerical grades   junior management   middle management

semi-skilled grades   ~~senior management~~   skilled grades

supervisory grades   unskilled grades

White-collar grades

1   *senior management*

2   _____

3   _____

4   _____

Blue-collar grades

5   _____

6   _____

7   _____

8   _____

There are eight **layers** or **levels** in the organization chart of this company. A company with only a few levels has a **flat organization**. A company with a lot of levels is often very **hierarchical** because decisions have to travel through several layers.

White-collar workers often work in offices, banks, etc. They work in management or administration.

Blue-collar workers often work with their hands, for example on the production line in a factory.

13 The organization chart

Read this short presentation of the management team of this British company. Then write the correct letters (a–n) in the right places in the organization chart.

At the top of the company, the Chairman of the Board [a] is responsible to the shareholders and the day-to-day running is the responsibility of the Chief Executive Officer (CEO) [b], who also has a seat on the Board.

Five directors form the senior management committee of the company. Going from left to right on the organization chart, we start with the Director of Finance [c], who runs his division with his Deputy [d].

Then we have the Director of Operations [e], who is responsible for production and logistics. The Factory Manager [f] answers directly to him.

Next we have the Director of Marketing [g], who is also responsible for sales so the National Sales Manager [h] reports to him on the activities of the whole sales team, which is divided into two regions, north and south, each managed by a regional sales manager [i; j].

The Director of Human Resources [k] has a Training and Development Manager [l] and a Compensation and Benefits Manager [m], who look after the day-to-day running of her department.

Finally, the Director of Research and Development [n] runs a small but important division of the company. She too reports directly to the CEO.

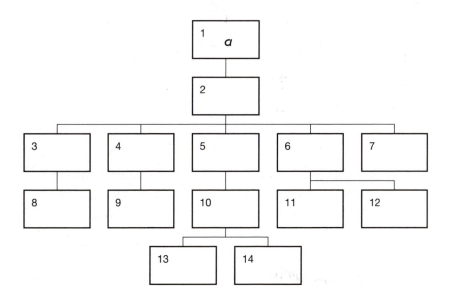

14 Departments

The organization is in trouble. Match the problems (a–l) with the correct departments (1–12).

1	Distribution	_e_	7	Telephone After-sales	_____
2	Personnel	_____	8	Marketing	_____
3	Research	_____	9	Reception	_____
4	Finance	_____	10	Switchboard	_____
5	Public Relations	_____	11	Information Technology	_____
6	Production	_____	12	Quality	_____

a
> One of the robots on the assembly line has stopped working.

b
> Cash flow is much worse than I thought.

c
> There's a national newspaper on the phone. They want to talk about water pollution near the factory.

d
> There's something wrong with the network: all the screens have gone blank.

e
> We have ten lorries waiting outside the main warehouse and there's nothing to put in them.

f
> The unions have just asked for another 10%.

g

If we don't start producing some more useful ideas soon, they'll close down the laboratory.

h

Last month, there were problems with 0.31% of the bottles. This month I want that figure to be zero.

i

I'm very sorry, madam. We certainly asked the taxi to be here at three o'clock. I'll call them again immediately.

j

The latest survey shows that the majority of 18- to 25-year-old women think our perfume smells terrible.

k

I'm very sorry, sir. I've tried to reach his secretary several times but there's no reply.

l

If this doesn't work, I'll send an engineer to you this afternoon.

In **production and distribution**, modern manufacturing is becoming very complex. **Parts** can come into the factory from many different suppliers and **finished goods** then have to go to customers. Managing this process is called managing the **supply chain**.

Making products or providing services of good *quality* – that is, to a high standard – should be important for every company. Some companies have quality managers. But even if there is a quality manager, quality is everyone's responsibility.

People in **telephone after-sales** help callers who may have problems with products they have bought. For example, if you buy a computer and you don't understand how to make it work, someone in telephone after-sales will tell you what to do.

15 Locations

Ursula is telling her visitors about where the company is located. Fill in the spaces in the sentences below.

> factories   ~~head office~~   local agents
> local offices   office   plant   regional headquarters
> research and development centres   training centres   warehouses

Our (1) _____ *head office* _____ is in London. This is where most of our senior managers work. We also have four (2) _____ : in Singapore, serving Asia; in Boston, Massachusetts, serving the whole of North America; in Buenos Aires for South America; and in Zurich, for Europe, Africa and the Middle East. We have (3) _____ in seventeen other countries, and in countries where we do not have our own people we usually have (4) _____ .

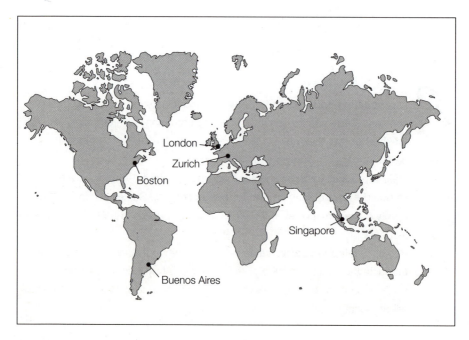

Of course, we make a wide range of products but recently we have closed some (5) _____ and reduced the number of products being made at others. However, distribution is still as local as possible and we have (6) _____ , depots and distribution centres in almost every country in which we operate.

We have also closed some of the smaller (7) _____ and moved many of our best scientists and technicians to two major centres in France and the United States.

We think that staff development is essential to our present and future success and we run more than 5,000 courses for our employees in the fifty (8) _____ which we have across the world.

Well, that's all I want to say about our presence worldwide. Now, if you would like to follow me, first of all I'll show you my (9) _____ and then we'll start the tour of the (10) _____ .

You can talk about your company's **head office** or your company's **headquarters**. But note that headquarters can be singular or plural:
Our headquarters is in Warsaw.
Our headquarters are in Warsaw.

16 Ownership

Fill in the missing words in the sentences below. Choose from the following:

> ~~family company~~   hostile takeover   joint venture   merger
> parent company   principal shareholders   privatized   stakeholders
> state-owned   subsidiaries   takeover

1 Rich & Bright was started by Sam Rich and his brother-in-law, Charlie Bright, fifty years ago. It was a successful _family company_ .

2 But the Socialist Party won an election and the government nationalized the company. It was now managed by a government department. It was _____ .

3 Then the Christian Democrats won an election. The new government sold R & B. It was _____ .

4 But by this time both Sam and Charlie had died. The new owners were banks and pension funds. They were the

_____ .

5 Of course, many more people – managers, employees and their families, and clients – also had an interest in the success of the company. These were the _____ .

6 The new management decided to turn some of the business units into separate companies. They became _____ .

7 R & B kept a majority shareholding in all of them. It was the

_____ .

8 Then the American giant, Monsterbuck, suggested that the two companies work in partnership on a new product. They proposed a _____ .

9   But everyone knew that Monsterbuck really wanted to buy R & B. Monsterbuck wanted a _____ .

10 The R & B management did not want Monsterbuck to buy the company. But Monsterbuck offered the R & B shareholders lots of money and won control. It was a _____ .

11 Now there is news that Monsterbuck and another American giant, Megadollar, will join together soon. It will be a very big _____ .

It will be very big!

17 The business bag

Empty a manager's bag and pockets or purse and what do you find? Match the pictures (a–k) with the correct terms (1–11).

1	tickets	*j*
2	credit card	___
3	keys	___
4	mobile phone	___
5	cash	___
6	chequebook	___
7	passport	___
8	business card	___
9	wallet	___
10	personal organizer	___
11	adapter	___

a

b

c

e

d

 Cash is made up of **coins**, made of metal, which you keep in your pocket or in a purse; and **notes**, made of paper, which you keep in your wallet.

18 Business travel

Complete the sentences with words from the box.

---

aisle   bill   check-in desk   connection   excess baggage   hand luggage
reservation   room service   seat belt   single   ~~tip~~   waiter

---

1   The taxi driver took me the long way to the airport. I didn't give
him a _____*tip*_____ .

2   I got to the _____ ten minutes before take-off.
Fortunately the plane was late.

3   I had a very heavy suitcase and two pieces of _____ .

4   The suitcase and one of the other bags were too heavy and I had
to pay an _____ charge.

5   I wanted a window seat but I could only get an
_____ seat.

6   The weather was bad and I had to wear my _____
all through the trip.

7   The first plane arrived very late and so I missed my
_____ . I waited three hours in the airport for
another flight.

8   At last I arrived at my hotel. They could not find my
_____ .

9   I wanted a double room but I had to take a _____ .

10   I went to the hotel restaurant but could not find a
_____ to serve me.

11   I went back to my room and tried _____ but there
was no reply.

12   In the morning I asked for my _____ . I don't
need to tell you: they had got it wrong!

19 Communications

Find words in the word square which match these descriptions. The words may run from the top down, from the bottom up, from left to right or diagonally.

1. It can weigh less than 200 grams and you can call your friends from almost anywhere with it. (6 and 5 letters)
2. It bleeps to tell you there's a call. (5 letters)
3. It connects computers round the world. (8 letters)
4. You can go here for information in text, sound and pictures about an organization or an individual. (7 letters)
5. The way for your company to buy and sell its products and services via computer. (9 letters)
6. A message you send from one computer to another. (5 letters)
7. A computer which you can carry with you when you travel. (6 letters)
8. A computer which you can put in your pocket. (7 letters)
9. A virtual company. (6 letters)

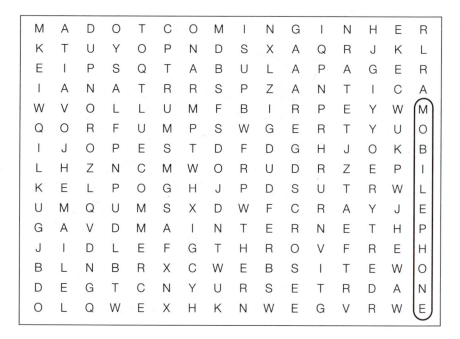

M	A	D	O	T	C	O	M	I	N	G	I	N	H	E	R
K	T	U	Y	O	P	N	D	S	X	A	Q	R	J	K	L
E	I	P	S	Q	T	A	B	U	L	A	P	A	G	E	R
I	A	N	A	T	R	R	S	P	Z	A	N	T	I	C	A
W	V	O	L	L	U	M	F	B	I	R	P	E	Y	W	M
Q	O	R	F	U	M	P	S	W	G	E	R	T	Y	U	O
I	J	O	P	E	S	T	D	F	D	G	H	J	O	K	B
L	H	Z	N	C	M	W	O	R	U	D	R	Z	E	P	I
K	E	L	P	O	G	H	J	P	D	S	U	T	R	W	L
U	M	Q	U	M	S	X	D	W	F	C	R	A	Y	J	E
G	A	V	D	M	A	I	N	T	E	R	N	E	T	H	P
J	I	D	L	E	F	G	T	H	R	O	V	F	R	E	H
B	L	N	B	R	X	C	W	E	B	S	I	T	E	W	O
D	E	G	T	C	N	Y	U	R	S	E	T	R	D	A	N
O	L	Q	W	E	X	H	K	N	W	E	G	V	R	W	E

20 Number crunching

Look at the spoken numbers in the box. Decide which sentence each number fits into, and then write the same number in figures in the sentence.

fifty-five	three-quarters
half seven	~~twenty-fifth~~
nought point nought three	twenty-three hundred
one quarter	two
seven thirty	two thousand and two
three double four oh four five six two	zero

1 Pay day for our salaried employees is on the _____ *25th* _____ of every month.

2 We do a major strategic review every two or three years. The last one was at the beginning of _____ .

3 Jimmy has saved a lot of money. He plans to retire when he's

_____ .

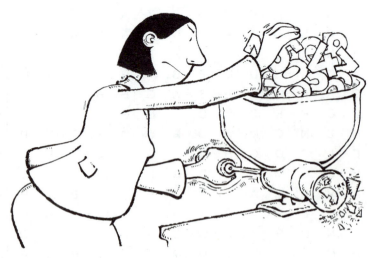

A lot of managers have to crunch numbers.

4   He also has a good pension scheme. It should give him about _____ of his salary after he retires.

5   We've reduced the percentage of damaged goods to _____ per cent of production.

6   We hope to achieve a level of _____ defects soon.

7   The timetable says that Charlotte's plane should arrive at _____ hours.

8   This is _____ . Can I help you?

9   The meeting will start at _____ in the morning precisely.

10   _____ ?! That's a bit early, isn't it?

11   Interest rates have gone up again – from 7¼% to 7½% – that is to say, by _____ of one per cent.

12   Sales increased by _____ per cent last year: this is a rather disappointing result.

A **number cruncher** is a person who or a machine which works with numbers and does a lot of calculations very quickly. A lot of managers have to crunch numbers.

If you don't know the exact number, you can say:

It's **about** *100.*

It's **around** *100.*

It's **roughly** *100.*

It's **approximately** *100.*

21 Describing people 1

Match the descriptions (a–m) with the personality adjectives (1–13).

1	tidy	_h_	a	works well, does not waste time
2	shy	____	b	wants to have a top job
3	self-confident	____	c	doesn't get angry when he or she has to wait
4	reliable	____	d	doesn't feel confident when talking to people he or she doesn't know
5	patient	____	e	trustworthy, dependable
6	demanding	____	f	thinks carefully before doing or deciding anything
7	nervous	____	g	arrives on time
8	ambitious	____	h	keeps desk, papers, files, etc. in good order
9	relaxed	____	i	calm, unstressed, unworried
10	cautious	____	j	has a positive feeling about him or herself
11	dynamic	____	k	makes other people work hard, often to a high standard
12	efficient	____	l	afraid, does not have a lot of confidence
13	punctual	____	m	energetic and (usually) successful

An **appraisal** is a description of your performance at work. Many people have **appraisal interviews** with their bosses one or more times per year to discuss the work they did in the last year and the work they will do next year. More and more **job interviews** and appraisal interviews are done in English.

22 Describing people 2

These pairs of words describe employee qualities and performance. From the words on the right, choose a synonym for each adjective (1–12).

#	Adjective	Synonym		Word
1	tidy	*neat*		**clever**
2	friendly			**timid**
3	careful			**easy-going**
4	intelligent			**acceptable**
5	shy			**self-assured**
6	reliable			**cautious**
7	relaxed			**adaptable**
8	self-confident			**neat**
9	flexible			**consistent**
10	systematic			**outstanding**
11	satisfactory			**dependable**
12	excellent			**warm**

André is a very self-confident manager.

23 Describing people 3

Write the negative forms of the following adjectives using the prefixes
un- (11 examples), in- (7 examples), dis- (3 examples), ir- (1 example)
or im- (1 example).

Adjective	Negative	Adjective	Negative
1 tidy	_untidy_	13 obedient	_____
2 organized	_____	14 reliable	_____
3 accurate	_____	15 predictable	_____
4 systematic	_____	16 friendly	_____
5 sensitive	_____	17 diplomatic	_____
6 patient	_____	18 trustworthy	_____
7 conventional	_____	19 tolerant	_____
8 traditional	_____	20 sincere	_____
9 convincing	_____	21 orthodox	_____
10 responsible	_____	22 honest	_____
11 efficient	_____	23 experienced	_____
12 secure	_____		

Herbert is a very traditional manager.

24 Business word pairs

Match the terms on the right (a–r) with their equivalents on the left (1–18).

1	headquarters	_m_	a	chief	
2	executive	____	b	plan	
3	human resources	____	c	products	
4	customer	____	d	sales revenue	
5	factory	____	e	position	
6	head	____	f	purchaser	
7	firm	____	g	correspondence	
8	manufacturing	____	h	objective	
9	Chief Executive Officer	____	i	plant	
10	turnover	____	j	deliver	
11	pay	____	k	manager	
12	buyer	____	l	production	
13	post	____	m	head office	
14	supply	____	n	Managing Director	
15	target	____	o	company	
16	letters	____	p	salary	
17	goods	____	q	client	
18	scheme	____	r	personnel	

25 Basic business words

Write one word in each mind map. Choose from the words and phrases in the box.

> business   customer   executive   financial   management
> ~~market~~   price   products   profit   staff

1   enter a new ~

market

a ~ study   a crowded ~

2   a high ~

a bargain ~   a competitive ~

3   gross ~

~ after tax   a net ~

4   top-quality ~

best-selling ~   a wide range of ~

5   a potential ~

a ~ complaint   an unhappy ~

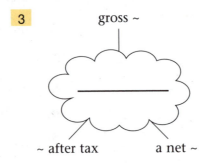
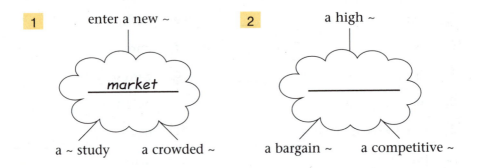
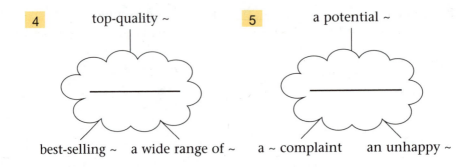

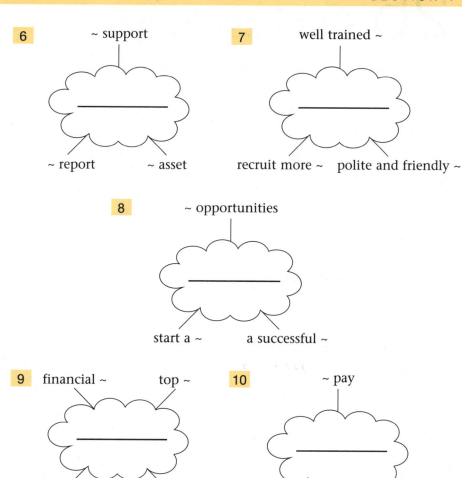

6   ~ support
    ~ report   ~ asset

7   well trained ~
    recruit more ~   polite and friendly ~

8   ~ opportunities
    start a ~   a successful ~

9   financial ~   top ~
    junior ~   middle ~

10   ~ pay
     ~ desk   ~ car

Learning single words is not enough. Learning word families like these will help you build better sentences, understand better how individual words work and speak better English. Always look for word families when you read and listen to English.

People use **mind maps** as a learning tool, to remember vocabulary and to brainstorm ideas. In language learning, you can use a mind map to remember which words go together. Put one word (for example a verb: *manage*) in the central circle and then show other words (for example nouns: *project*, *team*) which often go with it. You can then add adjectives which go with the nouns (for example: *difficult*, *challenging*) and so on! People with visual memories find mind maps especially helpful.

26 Business idioms

Read the sad story of Pedro Brown. Then match the idioms (1–12) with their meanings (a–l).

1	Pedro Brown was on the ball.	_f_
2	He had a good track record.	____
3	He had a good nose for a sale.	____
4	And he usually played his cards right.	____
5	But success went to his head.	____
6	He began to lose his touch.	____
7	He was always up to his eyes in work.	____
8	He started trying to pass the buck.	____
9	And then he put his foot in it.	____
10	The boss gave him a piece of his mind.	____
11	Nobody put him in the picture any more.	____
12	And in the end he was fired.	____

Pedro Brown was on the ball.

a	He began to have too important an opinion of himself.
b	He had too many things to do.
c	He made a big mistake.
d	He lost his job.
e	He was not told what was happening.
f	He was a clever employee, he knew what was going on.
g	He made the right decisions.
h	He passed responsibility to other people.
i	His job experience was good.
j	He talked to him very directly.
k	He started to make mistakes.
l	He was a natural salesman.

He was up to his eyes in work.

27 Business verbs

The company is in crisis. Below is a memo from the Chief Executive Officer. Fill in the missing words in the sentences.

> cut   deal   decide   ~~fix~~   forecast   launch   make
> play   raise   reach   solve

We have to:

1   _____*fix*_____ a meeting.

2   _____ with a very difficult situation.

3   _____ the problem of falling sales.

4   _____ agreement about exactly what to do.

5   _____ on a strategy.

6   _____ a profit next year.

7   _____ a new product very soon.

8   _____ next year's sales.

9   _____ the prices of our existing products.

10 _____ costs and staff.

11 _____ a different role in the market in order to survive.

 You can also:
arrange a meeting, call a meeting or **organize a meeting.**

28 Business word families 1

Circle the 'odd one out' in each of these groups of basic business words.

1	a) firm	b) company	c) enterprise	(d) manager
2	a) plant	b) factory	c) office	d) works
3	a) sell	b) make	c) produce	d) manufacture
4	a) client	b) customer	c) consumer	d) employee
5	a) salary	b) research	c) pay	d) income
6	a) manager	b) profit	c) executive	d) business person
7	a) export	b) division	c) section	d) department
8	a) assistant	b) desk	c) deputy	d) subordinate
9	a) timetable	b) plan	c) schedule	d) market
10	a) staff	b) personnel	c) product	d) workforce
11	a) choice	b) option	c) action	d) alternative
12	a) discuss	b) call	c) phone	d) ring
13	a) aim	b) target	c) reach	d) objective

29 Business word families 2

Write one word in each mind map. Choose from the following:

accounting ~~advertising~~ communications computer financial market production quality research sales

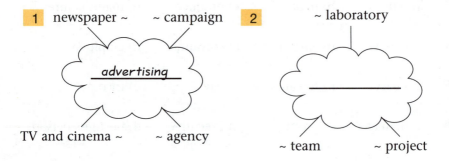

1 newspaper ~   ~ campaign
advertising
TV and cinema ~   ~ agency

2 ~ laboratory
~ team   ~ project

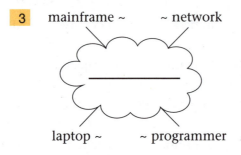

3 mainframe ~   ~ network
laptop ~   ~ programmer

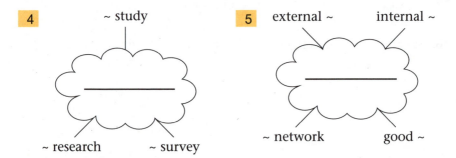

4 ~ study
~ research   ~ survey

5 external ~   internal ~
~ network   good ~

6

creative ~

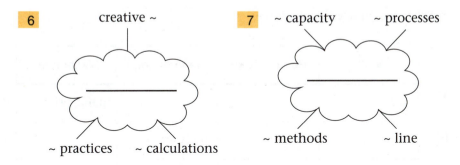

~ practices   ~ calculations

7

~ capacity   ~ processes

~ methods   ~ line

8

~ circles   ~ control

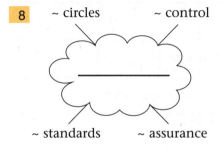

~ standards   ~ assurance

9

~ force   ~ figures

~ brochure   ~ rep

10

~ statements   ~ markets

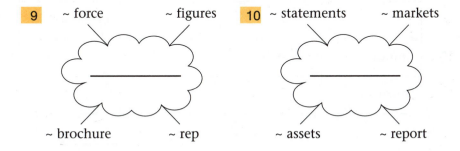

~ assets   ~ report

Creative accounting is when unusual but not illegal methods are used to make a set of accounts look better than they really are.

30 Business word building

Fill in the missing words in the table.

	Verb	Person noun	General noun	Adjective
1	manage			managerial
2			analysis	
3				organizational
4				applicable
5				competitive
6		decision-maker		
7		investor		– – –
8			production	
9				regulatory
10	inform	– – –		
11	persuade	– – –		

Informant and **persuader** are English words but they are not much used in business.

An informant can be, for example, a police informant – someone who informs the police about the activities of people s/he knows.

Fifty years ago, Vance Packard, an American writer, wrote a book called *The Hidden Persuaders*, about the advertising industry.

Someone who makes decisions is not a decider but a **decision-maker**.

31 Problem pairs

These pairs of words often cause problems. Choose the correct alternative for each sentence.

1 ECONOMIC / ECONOMICAL

    a) Prices are rising and the number of jobs is falling. It's not just a business problem, it's a general _____*economic*_____ problem.

    b) This car uses less petrol than the other one so this one is the more _____*economical*_____ .

2 TRAVEL / TRIP

    a) Zangief is doing too much business _____ and wants to cut the number of visits to foreign clients next year.

    b) However, he still has to make one important _____ to the agent in Singapore.

3 PRODUCTION / PRODUCTIVITY

    a) We will increase pay if the employees raise their _____.

    b) If we don't get another order soon, we'll have to cut _____ and maybe close a factory.

4 SALARY / WAGE

    a) We pay a monthly _____ by cheque to our white-collar staff.

    b) We pay a weekly _____ in cash to our part-time blue-collar staff.

5 EXPENSES / EXPENDITURE

    a) We have to reduce our general _____ : we must cut costs wherever we can.

    b) The sales manager has to cut his travel, accommodation and entertainment _____ : he'll have to stay in cheaper hotels and take his clients to cheaper restaurants.

6 PERSONNEL / PERSONAL

a) Smith has a _____ problem: his wife wants to leave him.

b) Smith's company has a _____ problem: their employees want a 20% pay increase.

7 INTERVIEWEE / INTERVIEWER

a) The person who usually asks most of the questions at an interview is the _____.

b) The person who usually answers most of the questions at an interview is the _____.

8 FOREIGNERS / STRANGERS

a) Our company has been bought by a German multinational. More and more _____ are coming from abroad to work in our office.

b) There were two _____ at the corner table in the restaurant where we usually go for lunch: no one had ever seen them before.

9 WHITE-COLLAR / BLUE-COLLAR

a) _____ workers work in the factory.

b) _____ workers work in the office.

10 ADVERTISING / ADVERTISEMENT

a) Our _____ budget is 10% less than last year.

b) Did you see the big _____ for a new Managing Director for Acme in this morning's newspapers?

11 LINE / STAFF

a) A _____ manager works directly on the production of goods or the provision of services.

b) A _____ manager gives support to the managers who produce the goods or provide the services.

12 RAISING / RISING

a) Prices are _____ at a rate of about 4% per year.

b) The company is _____ its prices by 5% this year.

32 Key phrases for business communication

Match the pictures (a–h) with the phrases (1–8).

1	Could you hold on, please?	*a*
2	Do you have any questions?	____
3	I'm very sorry, madam. I'll make sure this doesn't happen again.	____
4	How are you?	____
5	I'm afraid that Mr Fangio is unavailable at the moment.	____
6	I've divided my subject into three parts.	____
7	Let me take your coats.	____
8	There are several points on today's agenda.	____

a

b

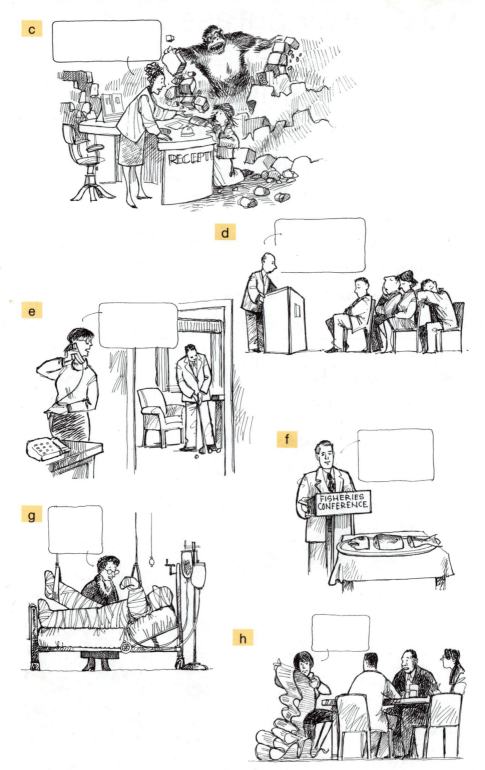

33 Internal communication

Business people communicate with each other in a number of different ways.
Match the pictures (a–k) with the correct terms (1–11).

1	e-mail	_b_	**7**	office gossip	____
2	phone	____	**8**	face to face	____
3	letter	____	**9**	intranet	____
4	fax	____	**10**	meeting	____
5	video conference	____	**11**	in-house magazine	____
6	notice board	____			

34 Presentations

Suzi Capra wants to make a good start to her presentation, so she has made a list of the things she wants to say. Unfortunately she has dropped all her language cards (a–j) on the floor. Help her to put them in the right order by matching them with the cues (1–10).

Cues

1	THANK audience for coming.	_c_
2	INTRODUCE myself.	____
3	Give JOB title.	____
4	Give TITLE of presentation.	____
5	Give REASON.	____
6	Give STRUCTURE.	____
7	Give LENGTH.	____
8	VISUAL AIDS I plan to use.	____
9	No QUESTIONS until the end.	____
10	START first part.	____

Language cards

a I plan to show you some slides and a short video during my presentation.

b So, first of all, let's take a look at …

c I'm very grateful that you could all come today.

d I'm going to talk for …

e If there is anything you would like to ask me, please would you wait until the end of the presentation.

f My name is …

g My talk will be in four main parts.

h The subject of my presentation today is …

i I'm the …

j I'm going to talk about this because …

35 Using visual aids

You have to show this visual aid to the people at your presentation. Can you say where each place is? Make complete sentences.

Example: *The main office is in the top left-hand corner.*

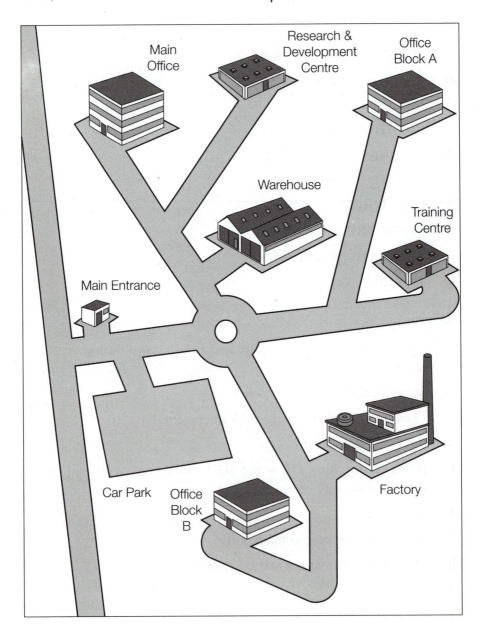

1	The main office is		the bottom right-hand corner.
2	The car park is	on	the left-hand side.
3	The factory is		the bottom.
4	The R&D centre is		the top right-hand corner.
5	The warehouse is	at	the top.
6	The training centre is		the right-hand side.
7	Office block A is		the bottom left-hand corner.
8	Office block B is	in	the top left-hand corner.
9	The main entrance is		the centre.

36 Meetings 1

Fill in the missing words in the sentences below. Choose from the following.
There are two possible answers for number 8.

agenda	any other business	chair	closed
decision	item	matters arising	~~meeting~~
minutes	monthly	point	room	start

1 It was a terrible _____*meeting*_____ .

2 It was planned to _____ at nine o'clock.

3 But no one had the _____ .

4 And no one knew which _____ to go to.

5 The _____ arrived at 9.15. At last we thought we could start.

'Thank you, everyone. That was an interesting discussion about how long the meeting should last. It's a pity we don't have time to discuss anything else.'

6   But no one had the _____ of the last meeting, so
    the secretary had to go and look for them – and to make copies of
    the agenda.

7   It took a long time to go through the _____ from
    the last meeting.

8   At last we got to the main _____ on the agenda.

9   We talked for two hours but did not reach a _____ .

10 There was no time for _____ .

11 The chair declared the meeting _____ just before
    midday.

12 Thank goodness it's only a _____ meeting!

Some useful vocabulary for meetings:

The **agenda** – the list of things to discuss.

The **minutes** – the report of a meeting.

The **chair** – the person who leads the meeting.

Matters arising – things to discuss from the last meeting.

Any Other Business (AOB) – the chance for people to discuss things
which are not on the agenda.

37 Meetings 2

Meetings have different kinds of objectives. Match what people are saying (a–i) with the correct meetings (1–9).

1	Meeting to maintain contact	*d*
2	Brainstorming meeting	____
3	Decision-making meeting	____
4	Discussion meeting	____
5	Annual General Meeting	____
6	Information meeting	____
7	Negotiation	____
8	Planning meeting	____
9	Problem-solving meeting	____

a
We've got to find a way of making the TX2 and the TX3 communicate with each other. Could the technical people come in next Tuesday?

b
We're meeting the unions on the 21st. We're going to discuss with them their demand for a salary increase for next year.

c
I'd now like to call on the Chairman of the Board to give us his report on the year's activities.

d
If you're in the country next month, come over and see us: it would be good to get a chance to talk and discuss how our relationship could develop.

e

I've called this meeting because I want to tell you about recent developments in the KG23 project.

f

OK, let's see how many ideas we come up with in the next 15 minutes. I'll write them up on the whiteboard.

g

The atmosphere on the first floor is terrible. Could we have a meeting about it? I don't know if we can get a decision without Cedric and Jan, but at least we can talk about it.

h

We have just one point on today's agenda: to decide on the launch date for Zakko.

i

Can we meet next Friday? We need to plan the next three stages of the AK94 project.

A **brainstorming meeting** is a more informal meeting where everyone should feel free to make suggestions and to give their ideas, in order to develop new ideas or to solve a problem. There are fewer rules and there may not be an agenda for this kind of meeting.

A **troubleshooting meeting** is a mixture of problem-solving and brainstorming, when everyone at the meeting tries to find an answer to a current (and often) urgent problem. There is more likely to be a chairperson, an agenda and rules for the discussion in this kind of meeting.

38 Meetings 3

Fill in the spaces in the sentences by changing the nouns on the right into verbs.

1 Meetings are good if everyone ___*prepares*___
for them very carefully in advance.   **preparation**

2 First of all, we have to _____ who
should be the chair.   **decision**

3 I _____ that Mr Power should chair
the meeting.   **suggestion**

4 I _____ that he is the right man for
the job.   **agreement**

5 He is the only person here who can _____
the situation properly.   **analysis**

6 He can _____ the problem if anyone can. **solution**

7 Mr Hong, please would you not _____
when I am speaking.   **interruption**

8 Next point. I _____ that everyone here
should get a 20% salary increase next year.   **proposal**

9 We must _____ for the next stage of
the project.   **planning**

10 Celia is now going to _____ the sales
figures for the last quarter.   **presentation**

11   I hate the weekly sales meeting. Archie and
Fatima always _____ all the time.   **argument**

12   I _____ with what you say. I think
Steve is the problem.   **disagreement**

13   We need to _____ again soon.   **meeting**

14   We have to _____ this question
in more detail.   **discussion**

15   So, I'd like to _____ what we have
said so far.   **summary**

16   Good. So who is going to _____ all
this to the Board?   **report**

Archie and Fatima always argue all the time.

39 Business trends

In business it is important to be able to talk about things which go up and down (like prices and profits). Write the letter of each graph (a–j) next to the correct description (1–10).

1	The share price reached a peak.	*i*
2	The share price rose slightly.	h
3	The share price went up steadily.	e
4	The share price increased dramatically.	g
5	The share price reached a low point and then recovered.	___
6	The share price decreased slowly.	___
7	The share price fluctuated.	___
8	The share price levelled out.	d
9	The share price fell rapidly.	___
10	The share price went down steadily.	___

a
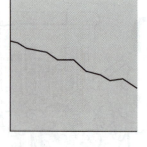

b

c
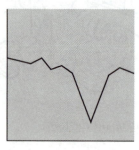

d
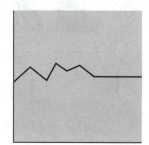

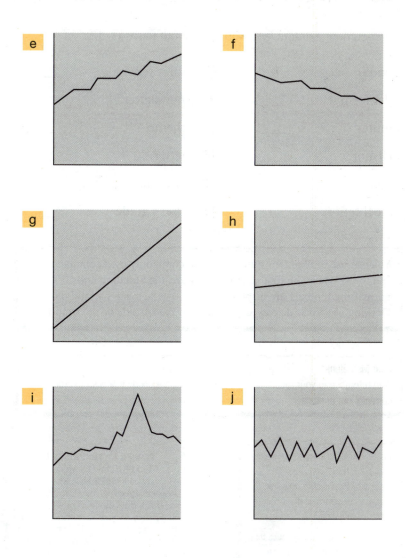

40 Business documents 1

Match the document extracts (a–l) with the correct terms (1–12).

1	agenda	_h_	**7**	sales report	____
2	order form	____	**8**	newsletter	____
3	minutes	____	**9**	memo	____
4	mailshot	____	**10**	letter	____
5	invoice	____	**11**	contract	____
6	annual report	____	**12**	user's guide	____

a
> You can use toolbars for quick access to commonly used commands and tools. When you first start the software, the Standard and Formatting toolbars are displayed just below the menu bar and the Drawing toolbar is displayed vertically on the left side of the window…

b
> Dear Ms Zelenka,
> With reference to your recent call, please note that the goods you wish to order are currently out of stock.

c
> To: All employees in H section
> From: GBH
> Subject: Restroom facilities for
>   H section staff
> Date: 28 July
>
> It has recently come to my notice that a number of employees in H section…

d
> **POWER ENTERPRISES UK CELEBRATES ITS MOVE TO FRISBEE HOUSE**
> Power Enterprises UK has just celebrated its move to new premises at Frisbee House, a beautiful listed building at the heart of the historic centre of Bristol and just a few minutes' walk from …

e
> **4** It was agreed that departmental running costs must be cut by 10%. Arturo will present his proposal at the next meeting.
>
> **5** Martha's presentation ceremony will be on 9 November. Everyone will attend.
>
> **6** The next departmental meeting will be on…

f

All prices are inclusive of VAT, postage and packing. If you wish to pay by Visa or American Express card, please complete the form at the bottom of the page. If you are not entirely satisfied with your goods, we shall be happy to…

g

This has been quite a good year for Flinco. Although the general economic situation was very difficult, sales increased by 7.3% and net income by 12.7%. At the same time, we reduced our workforce by almost 15% and continued to increase the range of products…

h

1   Minutes of the last meeting and matters arising.
2   The Zakko launch.
3   Problems in H section...

i

Figures for the Western region are generally good although the seasonal fall in sales of the XJ31 is stronger than usual and a major effort will be needed to bring sales up to target by the end of the quarter.
    Both Central and Northern have done well across the whole range despite ...

j

115 units of XJ45 at £23.50 per unit	£2,702.50
Less 15% discount	£405.37
Plus VAT at 17.5%	£402.00
Plus postage and packing	£360.05
Total	£3,059.18

Payment within 30 days of issue.

k

Dear Ms Bazalgette,

Have you ever dreamed of owning your very own holiday home in an exotic location? I am writing to tell you that thanks to Zangief Timeshare Inc., these dreams could become a reality!…

l

6.1 The SUPPLIER is entitled to modify the material ordered before delivery, provided such modifications do not affect the prices, delivery dates, quality performances or mechanical characteristics.
6.2 In all other cases, the PURCHASER's prior written permission is required to perform changes to the material.

41 Business documents 2

Write the types of written communication in the box next to the correct definitions.

agenda   annual report   contract   directory   fax   ~~in-house magazine~~
invoice   mailshot   memo   minutes   newsletter   order form
price list   sales brochure   sales report   user manual

1 it tells people – usually people inside
the company – about the life of the
organization   *in-house magazine*

2 a report of a meeting   _____

3 a letter sent at the same time to a number
of customers or possible customers, for
example about a new product or service   _____

4 a paper which you fill in when you want
to buy something from a company   _____

5 an internal message, usually from one
person to a group of people   _____

6 a list of things to discuss at a meeting _____

7 it tells people – usually people outside
the company – about the life of the
organization   _____

8 it gives information about the company's
products

_____

9 it tells you how much products cost _____

10 a book with lists of telephone numbers
or other information _____

11 the paper which tells you how much you
must pay when you buy something from
a company _____

12 a document which tells you about the
company's performance over the year,
including the accounts for the year _____

13 a legal agreement between two parties _____

14 a message sent by facsimile machine _____

15 it tells you how a piece of equipment
works _____

16 it contains figures on how much money
people have spent on the company's
products in, for example, a month _____

42 Visuals in written communication

Match the pictures (a–i) with the correct types of visual (1–9).

1	bar graph	*a*	**6**	organigram	____
2	diagram	____	**7**	pie chart	____
3	flow chart	____	**8**	plan	____
4	line graph	____	**9**	table	____
5	map	____			

a

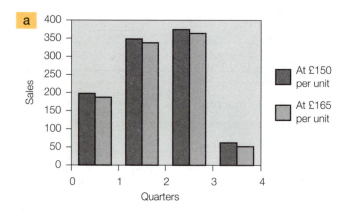

b

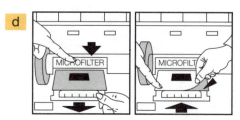

c

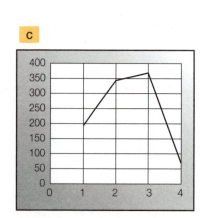

d

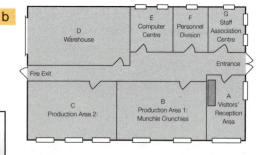

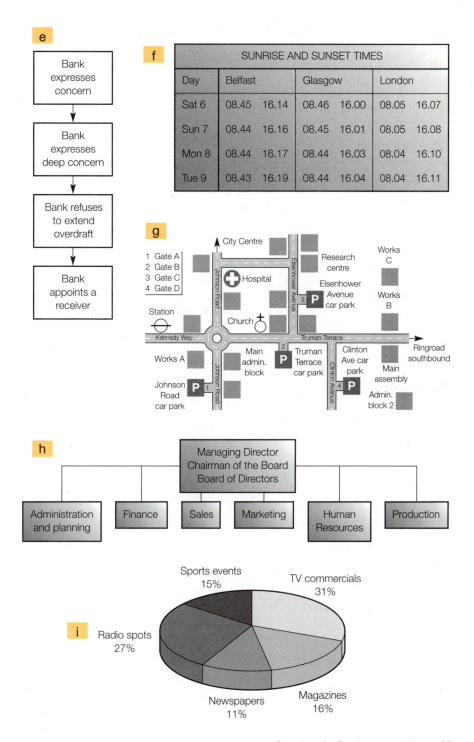

e

Bank expresses concern

↓

Bank expresses deep concern

↓

Bank refuses to extend overdraft

↓

Bank appoints a receiver

f

SUNRISE AND SUNSET TIMES						
Day	Belfast		Glasgow		London	
Sat 6	08.45	16.14	08.46	16.00	08.05	16.07
Sun 7	08.44	16.16	08.45	16.01	08.05	16.08
Mon 8	08.44	16.17	08.44	16.03	08.04	16.10
Tue 9	08.43	16.19	08.44	16.04	08.04	16.11

g

City Centre

1 Gate A
2 Gate B
3 Gate C
4 Gate D

Hospital
Research centre
Works C

Elsenhower Avenue car park
Works B

Johnson Road
Station
Church
Elsenhower Avenue

Kennedy Way
Truman Terrace
Ringroad southbound

Works A
Main admin. block
Truman Terrace car park
Clinton Ave car park
Main assembly

Johnson Road car park
Clinton Avenue
Admin. block 2

h

Managing Director
Chairman of the Board
Board of Directors

- Administration and planning
- Finance
- Sales
- Marketing
- Human Resources
- Production

i

Sports events 15%
TV commercials 31%
Radio spots 27%
Newspapers 11%
Magazines 16%

43 Business letters

Match the letters (a–n) with the different parts of the letter (1–14).

1	salutation	*e*
2	signature	_____
3	letterhead	_____
4	enclosures	_____
5	complimentary close	_____
6	final paragraph	_____
7	sender's title	_____
8	sender's address	_____
9	main paragraph	_____
10	website	_____
11	introductory paragraph	_____
12	date	_____
13	sender's name	_____
14	addressee's name and address	_____

GEA

Great Eastern Associates
377 King James Street
Edinburgh ED4 1MU
Scotland
Tel: 00 44 1301 567567
fax: 00 44 1301 567586
e-mail: infogreas@warmmail.com

a

b

c 7 February 2002

d Mr Felix Dubois
Banque Régionale du Sud-ouest
14 Route Nationale
24340 Mareuil
France

e Dear Mr Dubois

f Thank you for your recent enquiry.

g I enclose our brochure which gives you information about the services we offer and our prices. If you would like any more information, please do not hesitate to contact us.

h We look forward to hearing from you.

i Yours sincerely

j *Fiona McDuff*

k Fiona McDuff
l Partner

m Enc. GE Associates brochure

Great Eastern Associates
Partners: F. McDuff, R. McDuff, Z. McDuff, H. McKechnie

www.greas.co.uk

n

44 E-mails

There can be a big difference between the styles used for writing e-mails and for writing letters. Often – but not always – e-mails are less formal. On the next page is a table of different expressions used for writing letters and e-mails. Write each phrase below in the correct place in the table.

---

wbw

Re:

Dear Sam

Let me know if you need more information.

Hi Sam

Sorry about…

Please…

…attached

I should be grateful if you would…

Please accept our apologies for…

We regret to inform you…

Please find enclosed…

With reference to…

I'm afraid…

We are very pleased to inform you…

If you need more information, please do not hesitate to contact us.

I'm happy to tell you…

With best wishes

	Letters	E-mails
Greeting	1 *Dear Sam*	2
Topic	3	4
Request	5	6
Apology	7	8
Documentation	9	10
Bad news	11	12
Good news	13	14
Conclusion	15	16
Closing	17	18

45 Business forms

Mary McCann has filled in the form below. Write the following headings in the correct spaces on the form.

> Business address   Company   Date   Date of birth
> Extension number   First names   Job title   Marital status
> Place of birth   Postcode   Signature   ~~Surname~~
> Work telephone number

#	Heading	Entry
1	*Surname*	McCANN
2		MARY ELIZABETH
3		ACE PROMOTIONS
4		DIRECTOR OF MARKETING
5		65 KINKLADZE WAY, LONDON
6		NW6 7TL
7		00 44 020 7965 4200
8		372
9		14 MAY 1969
10		CAIRO, EGYPT
11		MARRIED
12		20 JANUARY 2002
13		*M E McCann*

Mary has filled in an internal company form. But if she had wanted a job with your company, which information could your company ask for? And which information could it not ask for? For example, in some countries, companies cannot ask if candidates are married or not.

46 The CV

Archie Wong's CV has got mixed up in the word processor. Help him to put the items in the right order by matching the information (a–j) with the correct headings (1–10).

1	Name	_f_
2	Date of birth	____
3	Nationality	____
4	Education	____
5	Qualifications	____
6	Experience	____
7	Current position	____
8	Responsibilities	____
9	Languages spoken	____
10	Leisure interests	____

a English, French, Cantonese

b British

c Military history, climbing, chess

d Loopers and Kylebrand, Chartered Accountants, 1988–91
Gabstock and Thring, Chartered Accountants, 1991–94

e Assistant General Manager, Power Enterprises UK

f Archibald Fitzpatrick Wong

g 8 September 1967

h MA in Politics and Economics 1988
Member, British Institute of Chartered Accountants 1991
MBA 1995

i General management of the company
Achieved 25% growth per year over the last four years

j Bootham School, York, 1980–84
Keble College, Oxford, 1985–88
INSEAD, Fontainebleau, France, 1994–95

47 Business functions

Match each group of words (a–o) with the correct business function (1–15).

1	Human Resources	_f_
2	Purchasing	____
3	Marketing	____
4	Training	____
5	Legal	____
6	Information Technology	____
7	After-sales	____
8	The Board	____
9	Finance	____
10	Distribution	____
11	Sales	____
12	Production	____
13	Research and Development	____
14	Accounts	____
15	Communications	____

a laboratory   test   scientist   trial

b parts   assembly line   shift   supervisor

c PR event   press release   company image   house magazine

d retail outlet   monthly figures   discount   commission

e capital   dividend   cash flow   share price

f recruitment   training   safety   employee relations

g invoice   bookkeeping   VAT   credit note

h network   screen   hard disk   memory

i questionnaire   mailshot   prospect   advertisement

j bulk buying   office supplies   order   delivery

k shareholder   executive director   non-executive director   chairman

l course design   student   needs analysis   timetable

m hot line   telephone support   complaint   24-hour service

n stock control   lorry   warehouse   packaging

o contract   patent   copyright   signatory

48 Finance

Match each quote (a–j) with the correct description (1–10)

a	We haven't put enough profit back into the company.	_8_
b	We don't have enough money coming into the company for us to pay our own bills.	____
c	We made more money this year than last year.	____
d	Last year, we spent more money than we earned.	____
e	We have to spend less on things like electricity, rent and postage.	____
f	At the moment we are spending more than we said we would at the beginning of the year.	____
g	We have decided to bill customers before delivery of the goods.	____
h	We think the figures for next year are going to be very positive.	____
i	We don't make enough money on the sale of each unit.	____
j	We can't do it on our own so we should ask the government for financial help.	____

Cash flow is poor.

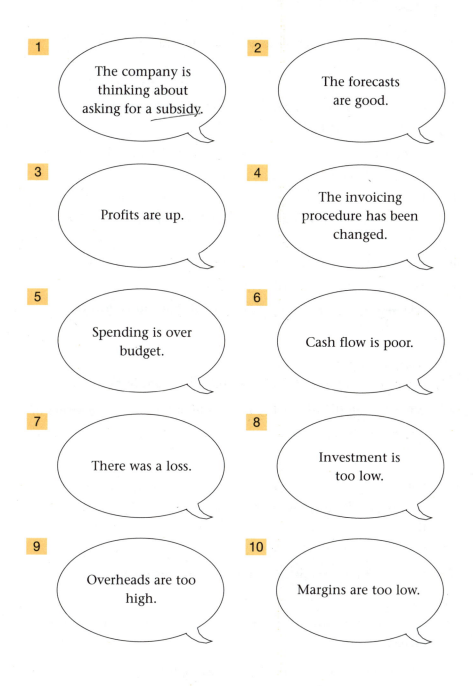

1 The company is thinking about asking for a subsidy.

2 The forecasts are good.

3 Profits are up.

4 The invoicing procedure has been changed.

5 Spending is over budget.

6 Cash flow is poor.

7 There was a loss.

8 Investment is too low.

9 Overheads are too high.

10 Margins are too low.

49 Marketing

Fill in the crossword. All the answers are connected with marketing.

Across

2 When a company has a new product, it has to decide on a
L A U _ _ _ date.

4 If you want to know what people think about a product, you do
some market R E S _ _ _ _ _.

6 The P A _ _ _ _ _ _ _ of a product is very important: the
company has to think carefully about how the product should
look.

8 The objective of advertising is to build up B R _ _ _ loyalty.

11 Some companies show the same television
C O M M _ _ _ _ _ _ _ in several different countries.

Down

1 You ask people to fill in Q U _ _ _ _ _ _ _ _ _ _ _ _ _ so
you can get information about what they want or need.

3 Where to sell the product is a question of P L _ _ _: another of
the 'Seven Ps' of marketing.

5 One recent advertising C A _ _ _ _ _ _ lasted for over a year.

6 P R _ _ _ _ _ _ _ of a product is the general process of
getting people to know your product, to like your product
through advertising and so on, so that they finally buy it:
another of the 'Seven Ps'.

7 One way to inform people about your product is to
A D _ _ _ _ _ _ _ it on TV.

9 You employ an advertising A G _ _ _ _ to create a product
image.

10 One more of the 'Seven Ps' of marketing is P R _ _ _: you have
to decide how much the consumer can pay for it.

 Three of the 'Seven Ps' of marketing are in the crossword.

The four others are:

Product – the goods or services a company provides.

People – everyone involved, from producer to consumer.

Physical evidence – anything that shows the existence of the company, e.g. its buildings, vehicles, website, stationery.

Process – the interaction between everyone involved.

50 Human resources

Match each group of human resources terms (a–k) with an appropriate heading (1–11).

1	Working conditions	_k_
2	Recruitment	_____
3	Training	_____
4	Management development	_____
5	Equal opportunities	_____
6	Pay	_____
7	Health and safety	_____
8	Employee relations	_____
9	Employment law	_____
10	Appraisal	_____
11	Pensions	_____

The interview.

a   retire   portable   period of service   contribution

b   accident   warning   inspector   first aid

c   strike   deal   dispute   agree

d   contract   tribunal   dismissal   union rights

e   time management   leadership   team building
assertiveness training

f   course   role-play   visual aid   self study

g   interview   objectives   performance   review

h   wages   bonus   commission   incentive

i   interview   apply   CV   headhunt

j   returner   flexible hours   crèche facilities   homeworking

k   duties   hours   holidays   full-time

Some companies employ a **headhunter** to help them find key personnel. This person tries to attract especially able people to a job by offering them better pay, more responsibility, etc.

A **tribunal** is a court of people officially appointed to deal with special matters. For example, a case of unfair dismissal may be heard in an employment relations tribunal.

A **bonus** is an additional payment on top of what is usual or expected. It may take the form of a share of a company's profits paid out to the people who work there.

Other terms for the word **crèche** are **day-care centre** or **nursery**.

51 Computing

Fill in the missing words in the sentences below. Choose from the words in the box. There are two possible answers to number 3.

> database   desktop publishing   directories   disk   drive
> folder   help   internet   laptop   modem   palmtop
> ~~software~~   spreadsheet   word processing

1 The screen and the keyboard are part of the hardware.

The operating system is part of the _____ *software* _____ .

2 One way to safeguard information in your computer is to copy files from the hard _____ to a zip drive.

3 To keep your files in order, you can make and keep them in different _____ .

4 If you want to work mainly with text on your computer, you need _____ software.

5 If you want to work mainly with figures, you need _____ software.

6 If you want to produce a good-looking magazine or in-house newsletter, you need some _____ software.

7 If you want to manage and manipulate large amounts of information, for example about your company's clients, you need _____ software.

8 If you want to use a computer when you are on the move, the best kind of computer to use is a _____ or a _____ .

9 If you do not know how to do something in a particular programme, you can use the _____ facility.

10 To be able to run CD-ROMs on your computer, you need a CD-ROM _____ .

11 For your computer to be able to send and receive information via a telecom link, you need a _____ .

12 You can use the _____ to get all kinds of information from computer databases all over the world.

The best kind of computer for people on the move?

52 Production 1: in the factory

Match the items in the picture (a–n) with the correct terms (1–14).

1	supervisor	____		**5**	packer	____
2	hard hat	____		**6**	assembly line	____
3	shop-floor workers	____		**7**	machine	____
4	overalls	____		**8**	machine guard	____

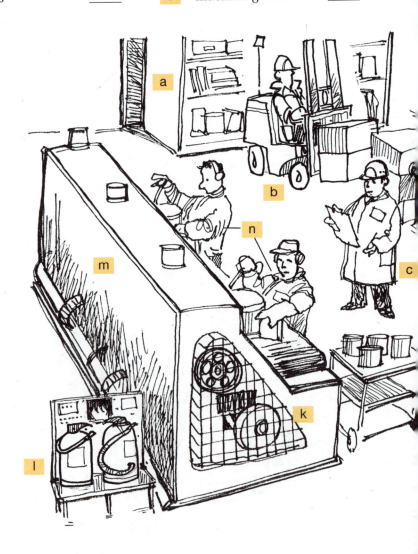

9	robot	_____	12	waste bin	_____
10	forklift truck	_____	13	fire extinguisher	_____
11	shelving	_____	14	safety notice	_____

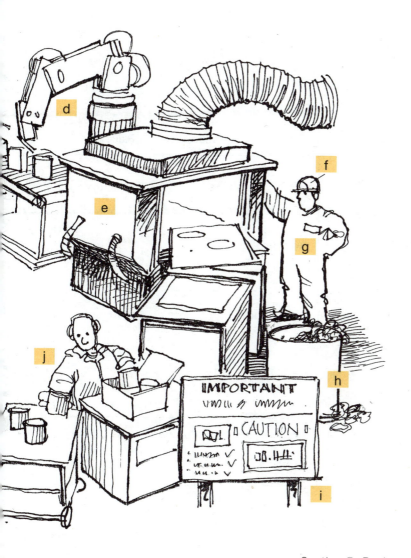

53 Production 2: from factory to home

The sentences in the chart below describe how goods get from the factory to your home. Match the letters in the chart (a–m) with the words or phrases they represent (1–11). Some words or phrases are used more than once.

1	a consumer		7	in
2	a distributor		8	makes
3	a manufacturer		9	sells
4	a retail outlet		10	through
5	a warehouse		11	transports
6	by			

Person	Activity	Goods	Preposition	Place
a 3	b	cars	c	a factory.
A wholesaler	stores	machine tools	d	e
f	g	frozen foods	h	road, rail, sea or air.
A retailer	i	televisions	j	k
l	buys	video cassette recorders	at / through	m

54 Business and the environment

What is the company's environmental policy? Fill in the missing words in the sentences below. Choose from the following:

audit	~~batteries~~	bulbs	green	packaging	photocopies
	plastic	recycle	scrap	suggestions	waste

1. In future, we should only buy rechargeable _____ *batteries* _____ .

2. We should _____ all the glass bottles and newspapers we use.

3. There should be different bins in every office for different kinds of _____ .

4. We should make sure that everyone separates paper from _____ .

5. We should encourage office staff to use _____ paper for notes and messages.

6. We should ask people to make fewer _____ .

7. We should always use long-life light _____ to light our offices.

8. We should reduce the amount of _____ on our products.

9. We should ask a firm of specialist consultants to do an environmental _____ of our activities.

10. We should encourage everyone to make _____ about how to make environmental savings.

11. We want to continually improve our _____ image.

55 Women in business

Sally Pereira has just been made Chief Executive Officer of Grotesko, a big retail chain. She wants to improve working conditions for women in the company. Match the features in her policy (1–10) with the descriptions (a–j).

1	Guarantee EQUAL PAY.	_h_
2	Introduce FLEXITIME.	_____
3	Improve MATERNITY LEAVE.	_____
4	Encourage HOMEWORKING.	_____
5	Allow more DAYS OFF.	_____
6	Increase the number of RETURNERS.	_____
7	Introduce JOB SHARING.	_____
8	Provide CRÈCHE FACILITIES.	_____
9	Provide EQUAL OPPORTUNITIES.	_____
10	Break the GLASS CEILING.	_____

Breaking through the glass ceiling.

a   Give employees more chance to stay at home if their children are ill.

b   Make it easier for women to move into senior management positions.

c   Give women more time away from work when they have babies.

d   Give employees computers with an internet connection so they can sometimes work from home.

e   Organize a facility where employees may leave their young children during the working day.

f   Give employees more freedom about the time of day when they start and stop work.

g   Encourage women who left the company to start families to come back to their old jobs later on.

h   Give women the same money as men for doing the same kind of work.

i   Give women the same chance to get jobs as men.

j   Allow partners or colleagues to share the same position.

In the companies you know:

Is there always the same percentage of women in senior management as in the company as a whole?

What is each company's policy on **equal opportunities**?

56 Business and the economy

Match the statements about the imaginary country of Zakaria (1–10) with their (similar) meanings (a–j).

1 There are 20 million people in Zakaria who want to work. One million do not have jobs.   *d*

2 Some industries are privately owned and some are state-owned.

3 Last year the size of the economy was $100 billion. This year it is $101 billion.

4 Prices are much higher this year than last year.

5 Banking, insurance and tourism, etc., are important to the country's economy.

6 But the production of cars, machine tools, white goods, etc., is still the most important part of the economy.

7 At the moment, the economic situation is bad. There is a danger that the economy will get smaller, not bigger this year.

8 Most working people have to pay about a third of their income to the government.

9 Today you can buy 10 Zaks for one US dollar. Last year it was the same.

10 Two million workers are members of labour organizations.

a The EXCHANGE RATE is stable.

b The standard RATE OF INCOME TAX is 30%.

c The MANUFACTURING SECTOR is larger than the service sector.

d The UNEMPLOYMENT RATE is 5%.

e People are afraid of a RECESSION.

f The GROWTH RATE was 1%.

g The economy has a large SERVICE SECTOR.

h TRADE UNION MEMBERSHIP is about 10% of the whole workforce.

i Zakaria has a MIXED ECONOMY.

j The RATE OF INFLATION is high.

The manufacturing sector

57 Outsourcing

Power Enterprises wants to concentrate on its core business. Match the
pictures (a–j) with the outsourced departments (1–10).

1	Mail services	_h_
2	Catering services	_____
3	Payroll administration	_____
4	After-sales service	_____
5	Security	_____
6	Cleaning	_____
7	IT	_____
8	Distribution	_____
9	Storage	_____
10	Training	_____

a

PE WORLDWIDE JAMES INGHAM 05/10/02
DEPARTMENT NATIONAL INS. TAX CODE PERIOD W 27
YEAR TO DATE PAY DEDUCTIONS
225.76B TAX
NI
225.76
NET PAY 195.64

b

c

3 POINT PLAN

d

Outsourcing happens when a company asks another company to do some of its work. Some companies like to employ people just for their **core business** – to work on the main products they make or the main service they provide. Some companies now outsource functions like human resources. It can often be cheaper for a company to get certain kinds of service by outsourcing rather than by employing more people directly.

58 Business initials and abbreviations

Jacqui has received similar e-mails from two different people. What do the initials and abbreviations in the second memo mean?

1 FYI *for your information*

2 CEO _____

3 VP _____

4 HR _____

5 R&D _____

6 AGM _____

7 ASAP _____

8 VAT _____

9 n/a _____

10 PA _____

11 OK _____

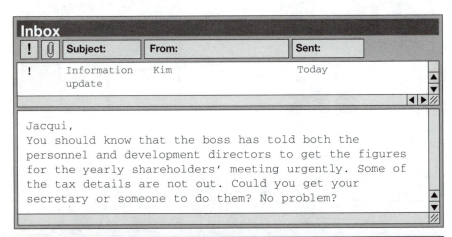

Inbox

!	0	Subject:	From:	Sent:
!		Information update	Kim	Today

Jacqui,
You should know that the boss has told both the personnel and development directors to get the figures for the yearly shareholders' meeting urgently. Some of the tax details are not out. Could you get your secretary or someone to do them? No problem?

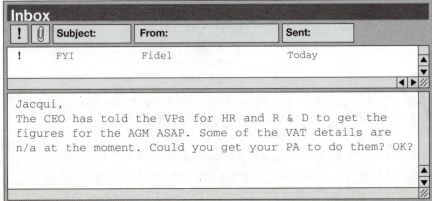

Inbox

!	0	Subject:	From:	Sent:
!		FYI	Fidel	Today

Jacqui,
The CEO has told the VPs for HR and R & D to get the figures for the AGM ASAP. Some of the VAT details are n/a at the moment. Could you get your PA to do them? OK?

59 From first to last

There are three verbs in each of the groups below. First, match each group of verbs with a noun in the table. Then write the verbs in the right order in the table from what happens first to what happens last.

1	start up	complete	manage	_f_
2	sell off	run	set up	_____
3	discuss	solve	identify	_____
4	negotiate	propose	sign	_____
5	test	research	launch	_____
6	set	meet	work to	_____
7	postpone	fix	hold	_____
8	build	break up	lead	_____
9	receive	resolve	deal with	_____
10	keep	fire	hire	_____
11	give	practise	prepare	_____

	First verb	Second verb	Last verb	Noun
a				a company
b				a meeting
c				staff
d				a new product
e				a presentation
f	*start up*	*manage*	*complete*	a project
g				a team
h				a problem
i				a deadline
j				a complaint
k				a deal

60 Your USP

What is your company's Unique Selling Proposition or USP? Fill in the missing words in the sentences below. Choose from the following:

> care competitors ~~employees~~ empowered experience
> flexible goal invest quality talking

1 Our __employees__ are the best trained in the country.

2 We look at what our _____ do, then we do it better.

3 We spend more time _____ to our customers than any other company in our field.

4 The _____ of our goods and services is <u>second to none</u>.

5 We regularly win industry awards for our levels of customer _____.

6 We have more years of _____ of working in this sector than any other organization in this country.

7 We have a more _____ approach to the needs of our customers than any of our competitors.

8 We _____ more in research and development than anyone else in the business.

9 All our people are _____ to take decisions on the spot about what is best for the customer.

10 Our _____ is to be number one in every area in which we operate.

 Every company has, or should have, a **USP**. Your USP tells people what makes your business different from every other.

Answers

a s t p i a

Test 1

1	in	6	for
2	in / for	7	in
3	in	8	on
4	in	9	on
5	on	10	for

Test 2

1 company
2 products
3 leader
4 share
5 employees
6 subsidiaries
7 customers
8 competitors
9 shareholders
10 turnover
11 profit
12 share price

Test 3

1	j	8	k
2	f	9	e
3	g	10	h
4	m	11	a
5	c	12	i
6	b	13	l
7	d		

Test 4

1 owner
2 Chief Executive Officer
3 director
4 boss
5 shareholder
6 investor
7 customer
8 supplier
9 leader
10 colleague
11 opposite number
12 manager

Test 5

1 salary
2 pension
3 benefits
4 stock option
5 car
6 expenses
7 health insurance
8 vouchers
9 bonus
10 income, rise

Test 6

1 CAREER
2 JOB
3 STARTED
4 LEFT
5 MOVED
6 PROMOTED
7 MADE REDUNDANT
8 JOINED
9 APPOINTED
10 FIRED
11 RETIRE
12 OFFERS

Test 7

1	k	7	i
2	f	8	g
3	c	9	b
4	a	10	h
5	j	11	e
6	d		

Test 8

1	c	9	f
2	o	10	i
3	d	11	g
4	l	12	a
5	m	13	n
6	j	14	k
7	h	15	b
8	e		

Test 9

1 main gate
2 identity card
3 security guard
4 main building
5 reception desk
6 receptionist
7 appointment
8 sign
9 badge
10 lift
11 floor
12 secretary
13 office
14 deal

Test 10

1	b	7	h
2	e	8	d
3	a	9	k
4	g	10	i
5	j	11	f
6	c		

Test 11

1	f	7	j
2	l	8	c
3	h	9	d
4	k	10	b
5	e	11	i
6	a	12	g

Test 12

1 senior management
2 middle management
3 junior management
4 clerical grades
5 supervisory grades
6 skilled grades
7 semi-skilled grades
8 unskilled grades

Test 13
1 Chairman of the Board [a]
2 Chief Executive Officer [b]
3 Director of Finance [c]
4 Director of Operations [e]
5 Director of Marketing [g]
6 Director of Human Resources [k]
7 Director of Research and Development [n]
8 Deputy Director of Finance [d]
9 Factory Manager [f]
10 National Sales Manager [h]
11 Training and Development Manager [l]
12 Compensation and Benefits Manager [m]
13 Regional Sales Manager North/South [i or j]
14 Regional Sales Manager South/North [i or j]

Test 14
1	e	7	l
2	f	8	j
3	g	9	i
4	b	10	k
5	c	11	d
6	a	12	h

Test 15
1 head office
2 regional headquarters
3 local offices
4 local agents
5 factories
6 warehouses
7 research and development centres
8 training centres
9 office
10 plant

Test 16
1 family company
2 state-owned
3 privatized
4 principal shareholders
5 stakeholders
6 subsidiaries
7 parent company
8 joint venture
9 takeover
10 hostile takeover
11 merger

Test 17
1	j	7	g
2	e	8	b
3	h	9	f
4	k	10	a
5	c	11	d
6	i		

Test 18
1 tip
2 check-in desk
3 hand luggage
4 excess baggage
5 aisle
6 seat belt
7 connection
8 reservation
9 single
10 waiter
11 room service
12 bill

Test 20
1 25th
2 2002
3 55
4 ¾
5 0.03
6 0
7 23.00
8 34404562
9 7.30
10 7.30
11 ¼
12 2

Test 21
1	h	8	b
2	d	9	i
3	j	10	f
4	e	11	m
5	c	12	a
6	k	13	g
7	l		

Test 19
1 MOBILE PHONE
2 PAGER
3 INTERNET
4 WEBSITE
5 E-COMMERCE
6 E-MAIL
7 LAPTOP
8 PALMTOP
9 DOTCOM

```
M A D O T C O M I N G I N H E R
K T U Y O P N D S X A Q R J K L
E I P S Q T A B U L A P A G E R
I A N T R R S P Z A N T I C A
W V O L L U M F B I R P E Y W M
Q O R F U M P S W G E R T Y U O
I J O P E S T D F D G H J O K B
L H Z N C M W O R U D R Z E P I
K E L P O G H J P D S U T R W L
U M Q U M S X D W F C R A Y J E
G A V D M A I N T E R N E T H P
J I D L E F G T H R O V F R E H
B L N B R X C W E B S I T E W O
D E G T C N Y U R S E T R D A N
O L Q W E X H K N W E G V R W E
```

Test 22

1 neat
2 warm
3 cautious
4 clever
5 timid
6 dependable
7 easy-going
8 self-assured
9 adaptable
10 consistent
11 acceptable
12 outstanding

Test 23

1 untidy
2 disorganized
3 inaccurate
4 unsystematic
5 insensitive
6 impatient
7 unconventional
8 untraditional
9 unconvincing
10 irresponsible
11 inefficient
12 insecure
13 disobedient
14 unreliable
15 unpredictable
16 unfriendly
17 undiplomatic
18 untrustworthy
19 intolerant
20 insincere
21 unorthodox
22 dishonest
23 inexperienced

Test 24

1	m	10	d
2	k	11	p
3	r	12	f
4	q	13	e
5	i	14	j
6	a	15	h
7	o	16	g
8	l	17	c
9	n	18	b

Test 25

1 market
2 price
3 profit
4 products
5 customer
6 financial
7 staff
8 business
9 management
10 executive

Test 26

1	f	7	b
2	i	8	h
3	l	9	c
4	g	10	j
5	a	11	e
6	k	12	d

Test 27

1 fix
2 deal
3 solve
4 reach
5 decide
6 make
7 launch
8 forecast
9 raise
10 cut
11 play

Test 28

1	d	8	b
2	c	9	d
3	a	10	c
4	d	11	c
5	b	12	a
6	b	13	c
7	a		

Test 29

1 advertising
2 research
3 computer
4 market
5 communications
6 accounting
7 production
8 quality
9 sales
10 financial

Test 30

1 manage
 manager
 management
 managerial
2 analyse
 analyst
 analysis
 analytical
3 organize
 organizer
 organization
 organizational
4 apply
 applicant
 application
 applicable
5 compete
 competitor
 competition
 competitive
6 decide
 decision-maker
 decision
 decisive
7 invest
 investor
 investment
 –
8 produce
 producer
 production
 productive
9 regulate
 regulator
 regulation
 regulatory
10 inform
 (informant)
 information
 informative
11 persuade
 (persuader)
 persuasion
 persuasive

Test 31

1. a) economic
   b) economical
2. a) travel
   b) trip
3. a) productivity
   b) production
4. a) salary
   b) wage
5. a) expenditure
   b) expenses
6. a) personal
   b) personnel
7. a) interviewer
   b) interviewee
8. a) foreigners
   b) strangers
9. a) blue-collar
   b) white-collar
10. a) advertising
    b) advertisement
11. a) line
    b) staff
12. a) rising
    b) raising

Test 32

1	a	5	e
2	d	6	f
3	c	7	b
4	g	8	h

Test 33

1	b	7	d
2	k	8	j
3	c	9	g
4	e	10	a
5	f	11	i
6	h		

Test 34

1	c	6	g
2	f	7	d
3	i	8	a
4	h	9	e
5	j	10	b

Test 35

1. The main office is in the top left-hand corner.
2. The car park is in the bottom left-hand corner.
3. The factory is in the bottom right-hand corner.
4. The R&D centre is at the top.
5. The warehouse is in the centre.
6. The training centre is on the right-hand side.
7. Office block A is in the top right-hand corner.
8. Office block B is at the bottom.
9. The main entrance is on the left-hand side.

Test 36

1. meeting
2. start
3. agenda
4. room
5. chair
6. minutes
7. matters arising
8. item/point
9. decision
10. any other business
11. closed
12. monthly

Test 37

1	d	6	e
2	f	7	b
3	h	8	i
4	g	9	a
5	c		

Test 38

1. prepares
2. decide
3. suggest
4. agree
5. analyse
6. solve
7. interrupt
8. propose
9. plan
10. present
11. argue
12. disagree
13. meet
14. discuss
15. summarize
16. report

Test 39

1	i	6	f
2	h	7	j
3	e	8	d
4	g	9	b
5	c	10	a

Test 40

1	h	7	i
2	f	8	d
3	e	9	c
4	k	10	b
5	j	11	l
6	g	12	a

Test 41

1. in-house magazine
2. minutes
3. mailshot
4. order form
5. memo
6. agenda
7. newsletter
8. sales brochure
9. price list
10. directory
11. invoice
12. annual report
13. contract
14. fax
15. user manual
16. sales report

Test 42

1	a	6	h
2	d	7	i
3	e	8	b
4	c	9	f
5	g		

Test 43

1	e	8	b
2	j	9	g
3	a	10	n
4	m	11	f
5	i	12	c
6	h	13	k
7	l	14	d

Test 44

1 Dear Sam
2 Hi Sam
3 With reference to...
4 Re:
5 I should be grateful if you would...
6 Please...
7 Please accept our apologies for...
8 Sorry about...
9 Please find enclosed...
10 ...attached
11 We regret to inform you...
12 I'm afraid...
13 We are very pleased to inform you...
14 I'm happy to tell you...
15 If you need more information, please do not hesitate to contact us.
16 Let me know if you need more information.
17 With best wishes
18 wbw

Test 45

1 surname
2 first names
3 company
4 job title
5 business address
6 postcode
7 work telephone number
8 extension number
9 date of birth
10 place of birth
11 marital status
12 date
13 signature

Test 46

1	f	6	d
2	g	7	e
3	b	8	i
4	j	9	a
5	h	10	c

Test 47

1	f	9	e
2	j	10	n
3	i	11	d
4	l	12	b
5	o	13	a
6	h	14	g
7	m	15	c
8	k		

Test 48

a	8	f	5
b	6	g	4
c	3	h	2
d	7	i	10
e	9	j	1

Test 49

Across

2 LAUNCH
4 RESEARCH
6 PACKAGING
8 BRAND
11 COMMERCIALS

Down

1 QUESTIONNAIRES
3 PLACE
5 CAMPAIGN
6 PROMOTION
7 ADVERTISE
9 AGENCY
10 PRICE

Test 50

1	k	7	b
2	i	8	c
3	f	9	d
4	e	10	g
5	j	11	a
6	h		

Test 51

1 software
2 disk
3 directories
4 word processing
5 spreadsheet
6 desktop publishing
7 database
8 laptop, palmtop
9 help
10 drive
11 modem
12 internet

Test 52

1	c	8	k
2	f	9	d
3	n	10	b
4	g	11	a
5	j	12	h
6	m	13	l
7	e	14	i

Test 53

a	3	h	6
b	8	i	9
c	7	j	10
d	7	k	4
e	5	l	1
f	2	m	4
g	11		

Test 54

1 batteries
2 recycle
3 waste
4 plastic
5 scrap
6 photocopies
7 bulbs
8 packaging
9 audit
10 suggestions
11 green

Test 55

1	h	6	g
2	f	7	j
3	c	8	e
4	d	9	i
5	a	10	b

Test 56

1	d	6	c
2	i	7	e
3	f	8	b
4	j	9	a
5	g	10	h

Test 57

1	h	6	j
2	g	7	b
3	a	8	d
4	i	9	e
5	f	10	c

Test 58

1 for your information
2 Chief Executive Officer
3 Vice President
4 Human Resources
5 Research and Development
6 Annual General Meeting
7 as soon as possible
8 Value Added Tax
9 not available
10 Personal Assistant
11 Okay? Alright?

Test 59

1	f	7	b
2	a	8	g
3	h	9	j
4	k	10	c
5	d	11	e
6	i		

a set up → run → sell off a company
b fix → postpone → hold a meeting
c hire → keep → fire staff
d research → test → launch a new product
e prepare → practise → give a presentation
f start up → manage → complete a project
g build → lead → break up a team
h identify → discuss → solve a problem
i set → work to → meet a deadline
j receive → deal with → resolve a complaint
k propose → negotiate → sign a deal

Test 60

1 employees
2 competitors
3 talking
4 quality
5 care
6 experience
7 flexible
8 invest
9 empowered
10 goal

Word list

The numbers after entries are the tests in which they appear.

responsible for 1
retail outlet 53
retire 6
returner 55
right-hand side 35
ring 28
ring binder 8
rise 5
rise slightly 39
rising 31
robot 52
room 36
room service 18
roughly 20
ruler 8
run 59

S
safety notice 52
salary 5, 24, 28, 31
sales 29, 47
sales brochure 41
sales director 11
sales report 40, 41
sales revenue 24
salutation 43
satisfactory 22
scanner 7
schedule 28
scheme 24
scissors 8
scrap 54
screen 7
seat belt 18
secretary 9, 11
section 28
secure 23
security 57
security guard 9
self-assured 22
self-confident 21, 22
sell 28, 53
sell off 59
semi-skilled grade 12
sender's address 43
sender's name 43
sender's title 43
senior management 12
sensitive 23
service sector 56
set 59
set up 59
seven thirty 20
share 2
shareholder 2, 4
share price 2, 39, 47
shelving 52
shop-floor worker 52
showroom 10

shy 21, 22
sign 9, 59
signature 43, 44
sincere 23
single 18
skilled grade 12
software 51
solution 38
solve 27, 59
spreadsheet 51
staff 25, 28, 31, 59
stakeholder 16
stapler 8
staples 8
start 6, 36
starting 44
start up 59
state-owned 16
stock option 5
storage 57
stranger 31
subordinate 4, 28
subsidiary 2, 16
subsidy 48
suggestion 38, 54
summary 38
superior 4
supervisor 52
supervisory grade 12
supplier 4
supply 24
supply chain 14
surname 43
switchboard 14
systematic 22, 23

T
table 42
take 3
takeover 16
talking 60
target 25, 28
team 59
telephone after-sales 14
test 59
three double four oh four five
    six two 20
three-quarters 20
through 53
ticket 17
tidy 21, 22, 23
timetable 28
timid 22
tip 18
tolerant 23
top 35
track record 31
trade fair 10
trade union membership 56

traditional 23
training 47, 50, 57
training and development
    manager 13
training centre 10, 15
transport 53
travel 31
tribunal 50
trip 31
troubleshooting meeting 37
trustworthy 23
turnover 2, 24
twenty-fifth 20
twenty-three hundred hours
    20
two 20
two thousand and two 20

U
unemployment rate 56
unique selling proposition
    (USP) 60
unskilled grade 12
user's guide 40
user manual 41

V
Value Added Tax (VAT) 58
Vice President (VP) 58
video conference 33
voucher 5

W
wage 31
waiter 18
wallet 17
warehouse 10, 15, 53
warm 22
waste 54
waste bin 52
waste paper bin 8
web camera 7
website 20, 44
white-collar 31
white-collar worker 12
with best wishes (wbw) 00
word processing 51
work for 1
workforce 28, 40
work in 1
work on 1
work telephone number 45
work to 59
working conditions 50
works 28
write 3

Z
zero 20